BUILDING A LEGACY

BUILDING A LEGACY

AVERY NIGHTINGALE

CONTENTS

1 Introduction   1

2 Section 1: Understanding Family Values   3

3 Section 2: Instilling Family Values   7

4 Section 3: Nurturing Strong Relationships   13

5 Section 4: Passing Down Traditions and Customs   19

6 Section 5: Fostering Personal Growth and Success   23

7 Section 6: Balancing Work and Family Life   29

8 Section 7: Overcoming Challenges and Adversities   33

9 Section 8: Sustaining the Legacy   37

10 Conclusion   41

Introduction

Consequently, we believe this is an especially appropriate time to question why one generation should leave much in savings to the next and then why the individuals who move into the next generation. As understanding of these model-building benefits by communities wanting to increase their generational wealth, they also have implications for governments. The importance of inheritance as a wealth development bridge from one generation to the next makes it indeed a serious national issue. Governments therefore should do what they can to provide a climate in which intergenerational wealth inheritance may thrive. They should introduce inheritance tax regimes that serve to protect these bequests. Hyperbolic discounting in a one-good model with durable consumption goods has generated promising reasoning for the existence of rich productive beneficent dynasties throughout generations.

Improved health and greater longevity are leading investors to develop a more sophisticated perspective about money, wealth, and inheritance. The perceived role and responsibility of existing and future inheritors is changing rapidly. With more of life spilling over into those post-age 65, the role and responsibility of existing and future inheritors in the societies where the traditions are the wealth would have profound implications. Families are often active in at least some dimensions of expected and intended inheritance. The systems within societies structure wealth inheritance flows. The practitioners are currently not well staffed to provide personalized advice on inheritance matters to existing and prospective inheritor families, who themselves should be marvelously well-placed to benefit from and contribute to the research and development of models with the potential to be of great expected practical significance.

CHAPTER 2

Section 1: Understanding Family Values

The family is looked upon to nourish and prepare us for life as much as our food nourishes our bodies. Mothers and/or fathers are the earthly representatives of the Lord, charged with giving to us daily examples of our Heavenly Father's plan for our lives by upholding the commandments of the Lord. Through family communions with God, the Lord instills in each family member a deep sense of understanding of spiritual truths through the Holy Spirit of truth, preparing us to face the storms of life while also developing in each a deep sense of care, concern, trust, and respect for one another. As Christians, parents should reflect the majesty of the love, concern, and forgiveness that the Lord has provided for us through the scriptures. By providing an atmosphere of spiritual training and the year-round practice of Christian rituals, we are allowing our families to keep committed to the Lord not only for social benefits but for the well-being of devoted believers to the Lord.

To understand why family values are important for the safeguarding of our Christian faith, we must first seek within God's word exactly what God expects of us as we travel our journey here on earth. Mark 12:30-31 states, "And thou shalt love the Lord thy God with all thy heart, and with all thy soul, and with all thy mind, and with all thy strength: this is the first commandment. And the second is like, namely this; Thou shalt love thy neighbour as thyself. There is none other commandment greater than these." The world will observe us to see if we believe in what we "say" we feel about God, and if they find that we believe, they also will believe and those the believers may come to know that we are the children of the most High and may desire to follow us.

2.1. The Importance of Family Values

The importance of family values can hardly be overstated. They can strengthen relationships and encourage communication when silence would be easier. They can link generations and help to maintain the rituals and culture of a people. They provide parents with a compass to guide their children successfully through life. Simply put, society does not exist in a vacuum, and younger members of it will not succeed without being instilled with these social values through family. One way that people can more deeply understand and appreciate the lasting legacy of conscientious parenting is to become familiar with immigrant families who left their country behind, not simply to seek economic opportunity, but to protect religious freedom, traditional values – coincidentally family values – and give their children the opportunity for a great life through discipline and a work ethic. A Lacayo family equivalent was none other than the Audubon's – this Frenchman arriving in the Americas found fertile ground for art, architecture, and ornithology learning, achievements that may not have been possible from within mother France's borders during a time of complex power dynamics and government, all of which did not generally favor the Jews.

Despite being nurtured in a loud and large Spanish family, the importance of extended family members and the unique bond among the women is embedded in my DNA. My mother raised me on her own, yet I was never without the love and support of grandparents, uncles and aunts, cousins, and family friends - all crucial to forming my character and becoming the man I am. A loving and supportive family does a lot more than simply allow children to grow up happy, healthy, and loved. Children who feel connected to those within the four walls of their home learn how to bond with others outside those walls, leading to a deeper understanding of and capability for creating healthy relationships with friends, and later colleagues and romantic interests. They're able to successfully negotiate the world outside the home and make valuable contributions to it because they are confident and self-assured. Most children who are encouraged toward education and living up to their potential academically have the benefit of a supportive family. When they feel secure and fulfilled, they're able to channel that emotional health in a positive direction and genuinely care about making significant achievements. This is one of the reasons that family ethic is an important part of every society, be it the United States, Spain, New Zealand, or any of the island nations in the Caribbean. In fact, some of the most exotic of these destinations feature family values as a highlight of their culture and are trips that may greatly benefit a family unit on holiday.

2.2. Defining Family Values

In today's dynamic, fast-changing world, clarity and universal understanding of these values are important. There is a misunderstanding that "to keep this good energy at home," creating family values is possible. It's hard for the members of the family unit to understand how to create quality values in the context of the eternal and sacred bond of love and mutual respect. In relationship dynamics, constructive feedback and general understanding is indeed a motivation produced among a family member to discuss disclosing family values. Their time, before the disintegration of family ties, should be appreciated by the general concept of family identity. How each person in the family can be defined and characterized with family attributes and attributes on the part of their partners. They also understand how being loyal to culture and tradition is important for gravitating the wonder of one another.

Family values are the source of human values. Our civilization is rooted in family and is the mirror of family values. It is the hidden source of all our good and evil. Our relationships with parents and through them, with God, morality, kindness, and mercy depend on and corruptive addictions, kinship, and family kindness. The problem now is to encourage, promote, or certainly maintain every possible way of realistic positive family values when faced with constant attacks on family life through large-scale negative media or failures in individual families fed by fantastic fantasies of sex. This is where family relations between people teach our hearts. Currently, the goal of family values, generated in the heart of each member of the family, is to improve family relations and to guide the child or future generation to become a morally upright family leader by transmitting family values.

CHAPTER 3

Section 2: Instilling Family Values

Kids are never going to remember every lecture you give about right and wrongness, nor the nephrology books that you give them to read. Instead, what they are going to remember are the memories in life that they have shared with you. This is why moral lessons in the form of stories will be the longest remembered. As a father, I will always remember how my mum told me as a child about a deceitful man who would run away after stealing chickens. She would emphasize the greed and how unfair it was to the owners of the chickens. Now, today, I look back and I realize she was actually giving me a short sermon and it worked! It paid off to hang out every evening with my mum.

So, how and what do you teach your kids to make them the best people they can be in this ever-changing and ever more complex world? You know, that starts in the home. It's all about instilling the right values in your kids and making sure they know that they can do anything they set their mind to. And your home is the best place to learn about this. You and your life partner must be the role models for your children that show them how to be honest, strong, judgmental, and knowledgeable. In this single house lies the magic that will help mold the child that will grow up to change the world. First of all, compared to their friends, parents are forever and will always be the moral compass of every child, so as a parent, be on your best behavior. The values that govern your house will be the foundation for every thought and action that he'll have in the future. So, a good character in children is the sum up of all the teachable qualities.

3.1. Leading by Example

Many of the principles that guide my team also define my own life. I pray every day for the wisdom and courage to lead my own life in a manner that will be honored by you and others. When I am asked to explain my team's success, I recount the persistence and accountability that comprise my beliefs and the bedrock of the program my father first introduced me to more than 40 years ago. I often discuss our commitment to helping each young man reach his full potential as a student, as an athlete and as a man. We work very hard to achieve the highest rankings and challenge the best teams, but emphasizes throughout our season that efforts to renew our spirit and to instill courage in the men he coaches and mentors has the best hope of success. We sincerely hope you will consider embracing these values and renewing your spirit as you watch a game at Nevada.

As parents, we want to see our children do better than we have done. We want to see them achieve more than we have achieved. From the very first time we hold our newborn, our desire is to show them by the example of our lives what pursuits are worth the effort, what causes are worth fighting for, and what teams to root for. It is my belief that the greatest challenge in our lives is to be who we say we are, to lead by example. I see these values in coaches and parents who give freely of their time, love, resources, and energy to help shepherd young people through this critical time in their lives.

With their leadership, integrity, honesty, and values, I know these young men will succeed after football, and long after I am retired from coaching.

3.2. Communication and Openness

The quest for openness appears to be a search for one of the values lost as a result of the deterioration of popular culture today. There are several other reasons why effective communication is taking the center stage in the lives of most families today, especially those who want their children to turn out well morally groomed. It is desired to avert the recurring cases of the "Well, it did not happen if parents only knew the truth." This study is a timely research on family values since the family has been experiencing declining values. Three forces that are primarily responsible for this malaise have been identified, which include the parents themselves, the school, and the peer influence. While these forces may try to be dominant, proper use of good principles of communicating among family members may be an antidote to the surmounting odds. Assistant here comes to the parent who instills the values, the child who puts into practice the knowledge acquired and who will soon become a parent, and to the society which will benefit from the values in their children or suffer from their absence. Religious bodies to which our quest for publication is a serious step in a research in progress on the effort of parents to teach their children family values. Some of the findings of the research made us extremely conscious of the importance of being open in teaching and maintaining values in the family.

Open communication is the foundation on which the other values groomed in a family stand. Without it, everything else comes crashing. It goes beyond father and mother talking to one another or mere interaction among children. It involves being transparent with one another, involving in each other's life, expressing concerns over actions of all, and showing unconditional love to all. Communication is the art and science of human care. It is an essential tool in expressing one's thoughts, emotions, and passion. Anyone who makes a habit of having continuous verbal and written dialogue develops not only emotionally but intellectually. But when it falls short, trust is threatened and the domino effect of resentment and self-blame may occur. Communication is essential to understanding another person as well as oneself. A child who can talk about anything can talk about drugs. Language fosters understanding and also creates barriers. It is a strong determinant in the level of knowledge possessed by the family, influencing the intellectual status of the children. The brute use of language leads to a sense of relationship tinged with schismari behavior.

3.3. Teaching Respect and Empathy

When I talk about respect, I'm not referring to etiquette or politeness, necessary forms of externalization of respect and appreciation for the needs of others. I refer to the most profound recognition of the common human need for happiness, especially those who face situations of extreme adversity, when the most violent challenges to human dignity are launched, carried out, and exalted. When I talk about empathy, I mean the ability to understand the feelings or needs of others, to recognize different modalities of love, the uterine ties of blood brothers, the affection of the chosen family. I'm not referring to feelings of solidarity, which are important to unite people in the demanding and grateful task of meeting the needs of others. I refer to the vital recognition of the inalienability of dignity, of the beauty of the struggle for happiness, and of the individual journey of millennia prisoners of the daily challenges and the essential need for support, guidance, and dedication.

No one is born respectful or empathic. We are born self-centered, affectionate, and curious. And from the first contact with the world, from the moment we open our eyes and start communicating, we start internalizing respect and empathy as we internalize our mother tongue. So the popular phrase "respect is born, it is not made" is not true. Respect and empathy have traits we admire and reproduce. We brothers are born rude and impose respect. But in a world transformed by the communication revolution, it has never been so urgent to teach young people the virtues of respect and empathy as now, or so dangerous to have them as the spearhead of education. This is the great legacy that makes it possible to build a respectful, empathic, and therefore more ethical world.

CHAPTER 4

Section 3: Nurturing Strong Relationships

Building a happy family is like going fishing. There's going to be some bait, a hook, a line, and finally some "fish." Here you'll find a number of very effective techniques that can be used to improve the relationship between brothers and sisters, parents and children, and between the extended family members. These techniques are the bait. When you use them, you are very likely to "hook" other family members with your love and helpfulness. Practice these principles and they will become a loving habit for you. This will help to keep the family members in your homestead looking for ways to help each other.

You love your brothers and sisters, but you fight with them every time you get together. You'd be happy to spend more time with family members, but they're so weird and different from you that you can hardly stand it when you're together. Sound familiar? In most families, conflicts are signs of problems. They're certainly not a happy thing. Yet it's not just possible, it's very straightforward to have family members who enjoy being together when they're together. You may say, "He's never happy with what we do!" Don't feel bad. Your family can have a better time when you're together.

By building positive, close relationships with your brothers, sisters, children, and parents, you will create a home where family members value and enjoy one another.

4.1. Building Trust and Support

In an ideal family, the support system never stops. Instead, it evolves into an ongoing safety net for individuals as they endeavor to achieve their dreams. At each growth milestone, it is reassuring to know that loved ones will be there. The role of encouragement and support should not be underestimated, and likewise, withdrawing support in response to pursuing goals considered beyond family expectations can be devastating to a person. Trust within the family setting confers a sense of stability and belonging, which is essential for individual growth and well-being. When members of the trusting family are assured of support from each other, they develop the confidence to pursue their goals with a level of purpose. This enhances the integrity of relationships within the family, and people tend to respect and value one another for their individual views, leading to a cohesive and bonded unit.

At the foundation of all healthy family relationships is trust. Trust is an intangible quality that is greatly valued in relationships in any context, but in families, it is essential for maintaining positive relationships. Traditionally speaking, your family is the support system that shapes your formative years, scaffolding early life's developments. In an ideal world, one should look forward to returning home for comfort and solace. With growth and independence, it is expected that the support role of the family lessens in making independent decisions and protecting individuality with less interference but continued support.

4.2. Quality Time and Bonding Activities

Bonding activities can be very simple and inexpensive. The only thing that is required is the willingness to spend time together. If your spouse enjoys cooking, surprising him or her by learning a few recipes that he or she likes can pave the way to deep conversations while cooking or doing the dishes together. The activities that families used to do together only a few years ago were those that brought everyone together and in the process chores were done and life's wisdom was shared. Today we have so many distractions, and many of the activities that our parents did to join us together as a family have been replaced by over-reliance on technology and solo hobbies. Set aside weekends or certain evenings for family board games and duration in the kitchen cooking together. Go for walks with your children at the park or spend the afternoon teaching them something that you are passionate about. A few months ago, in a bid to become more intentional about family time and strong connections that we would have in the future, a number of good friends made an agreement to once in a while have a sleepover just for the purpose of having the family moments that keep the bond going.

Families that are close are families that invest time in making memories that last for a lifetime. One of the legacies that you can leave behind is a library of shared experiences and precious moments. The "you-have-to-hang-out-with-me-because-you-are-my-relative" conversation is a popular family analogy. Ironically, one of the sets of people that we take out our bad moods on are our loved ones, and sometimes we have the habit of taking the most important people in our lives for granted. Time molds relationships, and the art of setting aside quality time for family and close friends is becoming rare. There are families that, except for Sunday morning rush and Sunday services, family members do not see each other throughout the week. If you want to build strong connections with the people you care about, you have to make a deliberate effort to do it. A close family is one that bonds together.

4.3. Resolving Conflicts and Forgiveness

Without minimizing the effects of conflicts in relationships, yet studies have shown that the way a relationship confronts and resolves conflicts can also be beneficial and can contribute to the health of a relationship. Effective conflict management enhances the relationship between the individual family members. If conflicts are not well resolved or managed, they could also become an impediment to the survival of the relationship, leading to the breakdown of such relationships. In order to deepen the capacity for relationship endurance, it is inevitable that individuals in a relationship should learn the art of conflict resolution. Conflict resolution articulates achieving and maintaining peace or harmony within a relationship. It seems to suggest that if this state is achieved, then the relationship is enhanced and becomes more resilient to the challenges that may inevitably erode families across time and space. Passive resolution of conflicts allows disagreements to simmer and boil until smoldered tension would erupt into an inferno of misplaced and displaced aggression. However, researchers argue that rather than use the conflict resolution strategies, it is imperative that family members acknowledge and tolerate their unique qualities and differences that contribute to their diversity. Such recognition and tolerance they observe would enhance collective family members' growth. Family members who have different views should learn to resolve their conflicts, accept their various viewpoints, and seek creative resolution that will foster harmony among the family. Failure to achieve harmony will definitely fragment the family.

Because of the inherent nature of people, relationships sometimes face challenges, which lead to conflicts. Though conflicts are part and parcel of relationships, researchers have, in their study, observed that very few people can effectively manage and resolve their conflicts. Thus, many conflicts remain unresolved, simmering and smoldering, while civility and harmony hang like the edge of an erupting volcano. Conflicts will also arise among family members because of the diverse interests, needs, and goals of the individual family members. Sander is of the view that conflicts within families are universal and inevitable because family life means close, frequent encounters and interactions which inevitably make differences more likely to spill over tension and conflicts and of course, there are a multiplicity of roles within the family setup.

CHAPTER 5

Section 4: Passing Down Traditions and Customs

With each next generation of family members, customs are handed down and can take on different meanings. Even as time moves on, some customs may be let go, while new ones are created. With the increasing number of migration and air travel, many inherited customs will be forgotten. But there are things like respect for elders, noble words of action, and community. Our customs can really draw our little families and then relatives together. If your family doesn't have any particular customs, create some. People of all ages and particularly children, who learn the importance and significance of the seasons through shared customs with family, school, and community, grow up to be focused and more understanding adults. Random events that don't happen regularly have no long-term significance and the reality is that many adults today had no traditions handed down by relatives. A great loss.

Moving on to another point, it is imperative to pass on traditions and customs, many of which may not seem relevant to today's society. It's these traditions and customs that can help stave off the negative impact of media. Are there certain days of the week that are family members' favorite or significant events/holidays? Is there a special meal that is shared in your family for every new baby? Do not think that you are silly for having family customs. They are what bond people and can give a strong foundation and understanding of cultural identification. Sadly today, the introduction of fast food has become the family dining table. With pizza, sweets, and soda, family members' health and behavior changed.

5.1. Preserving Cultural Heritage

Traditions create a sense of belonging to a group and identity, which means living people can connect with their ancestors, even if they have never met them. Family rituals, like family reunions, formal family meals, and family parties, are all rituals that can help preserve family values and ensure that future generations will have the same experiences. Many people believe that family rituals increase closeness among family members and that shared experiences will bring the family closer together. Family rituals also help children feel more secure and become more competent, which creates a safe and stable family environment. Children in a study indicated that family rituals give them a strong feeling of security that they can use to deal effectively with the challenges they face in life and thrive in. Sports that are shared as a family, and viewing sporting events together with the family, can be part of the ritual and create lasting memories and strengthen family ties.

When parents teach their children family history and heritage, the children gain a sense of history, family ties, and self-identity. Children develop a reservoir of knowledge about family traditions, beliefs, values, and social norms, and they also master the verbal skills needed to instruct, inform, and argue with others. Sometimes this means language, a local dialect, or a family or community language that should be maintained as much as possible and carried to the next generation. Our research has shown that the 5th generation (degeneration) of Cambodian French people, who first settled in France, no longer speak Khmer and have poor Khmer language skills. Retaining the language of the society helps members of the following generations maintain their ties with their former culture.

5.2. Celebrating Family Rituals

Children should accept their destiny by feeling they are part of a family with its own history, with precious things to offer and to transmit, without the separation between the generations being experienced as an impoverishment but as an opportunity for mutual enrichment in shared growth. Or, as the sociology of family rituals studies it, the time-space link, which is based on social organization and which "brings us back to concepts like rhythm, regularity, hierarchy which alone do not exhaust the significance and functions of ritual, but contribute substantially to the connection that is created between the individual and society, allowing the person to take into consideration different aspects of social activity".

The family intertwines the past, the present, and the future. This heritage of traditions, stories, values, obligations, and love pushes the family to continue, improve, and reach immortality. When considering the concept of immortality in the light of scientific advancement, what really gives the feeling of eternity is the family. This entity does not end with the "family, deceased, buried, forgotten." It is constantly reborn, rethought, renewed, and transmitted. Each celebration holds within it the force of this link, the certainty that the new members of the family will arise, and that the values that motivate this coexistence will be inherited. Generations follow generations, and the rituals that remain in the memory of the living are passing in an endless embrace that shapes, confirms, enriches, and spreads the story. It is a path that becomes sacred and that, before it is "destiny," is above all the concreteness of a well-defined individual and collective project. It is the family that creates unity and the path that transmits certain principles, in the hope 'of course' to receive the desired response in turn.

Section 5: Fostering Personal Growth and Success

For college students, who are learning who they are and who they want to be, these personal reflections and transformative moments are crucial. To foster their own growth, LSC-Montgomery donors created the Legacy Award to acknowledge and reward student mentors. The award supports faculty mentors willing to challenge their students, offer insightful feedback, recognize their development, and help them in both their personal and professional growth. Throughout the calendar year, acknowledged mentors receive updates on the achievements of their students. By forming a strong bond between beneficiaries and donors, the award encourages educators to follow the example of their patrons, people of integrity and leadership. The Legacy Awards intensify the confidence, talent, and potential for student success and for their educators offer inspiring teaching and scholar models.

Lone Star College-Montgomery currently measures its success by student graduation and transfer rates. While those are important indicators, the college is building a culture of conceptual learning that goes beyond the classroom, lab, theater or music hall. It is preparing future generations of thinkers, risk-takers, and innovators who understand and appreciate the value of individual inquiry, insight, and creativity. "The future of our world depends on the competencies of each individual to hold the tensions resulting from the interweaving of the striving for personal growth and success within the context of community," said Dr. Katharine Morris, professor of English and philosophy at Lone Star College. Mentors can serve as models of balance, people who connect their work to the world in meaningful ways. Generating future thinkers, innovators, and risk-takers isn't something that can be easily quantified. In the current atmosphere of performance-based assessment, attributes such as dedication, hard work, ambition, and passion cannot be measured. They are impossible to measure because they are the result of significant personal rather than external motivators. Instead of strengthening them, the system neglects them.

6.1. Encouraging Education and Lifelong Learning

It would seem that these difficulties that produced clarity of mind and resourcefulness, very few educational materials, created the moral configuration of completing the mother's advice, training the underprivileged and encouraging education and learning for life. Michael's confidence in people to come through for him on their privy times was instructive of this particular habit infused forcefully by the mother - being dependable, learning everything by doing them, to have become an autodidact, having great expectation, respect and trust in those you know or do not know. It is not true the saying that 'Success is the cause when mothers will pay their fresh bread makers more than their most influential doctors'. For although being given very much preference over the years, impacting the early years by different denominations and in later years, by experience, attending conferences and absorbing lectures on how creativity produces the very best in form and function with products or with the creative enterprises as well as the profits derivable, nothing seems to surpass the wishes of the mother.

Michael, the eldest of six siblings, was raised by a single mother while his father was establishing a business. The lack of material means did not subtract from the fact that every educational opportunity must be integrated from wisdom and spiritual peace for a purpose. All materials and technical means were perceived and made use of to reach the end in mind. While a rich friend can only afford to travel and be absent from school himself, he took notes of the lectures given on subjects they did in school, and paid him for his time which were so valued as he was the only or the best friend to draft the daily lecture notes.

6.2. Setting Goals and Ambitions

If you get to understand a little about an entrepreneur, you will probably discover they unknowingly used the philosophy of the 3H's as the methods they dipped into to create business value. Even objective job descriptions are found to promote inefficiency because they prearrange the objectives of the organization without putting into consideration context. The context of a position is set to change with time and technology and can sometimes pose challenges with substantial investments in professional development. Goal-setting theory focuses on the ways that leaders and managers can help staff set objective goals and performance standards. It does so because it aims to increase worker motivation and produce strong, positive organizational results. Goal-setting theory also emphasizes the need for goals to be tangible and feasible, and their significance will increase where there is engagement or direct feedback on progress.

Sitting down with family and coming up with a vision or mission statement about what is important to your family provides great insight into your legacy. It also gives you a clear framework in which to create laws and guidelines that you can implement to help maintain the values and vision you have. Laws (rules) should be internal, and those you can't control must become recommendations. This exercise also serves as a great team-building activity as you navigate through the visions each family member shares, which may not have been recognized in the past. This allows communication to grow in different directions and for the vision of a family to open up, just as it would within major corporations and the entrepreneurial world. This promotes transparency of thought and a more enfranchised individual, which opens a true understanding of teamwork.

6.3. Promoting Independence and Self-Reflection

I know that at the moment, I might be quite far from my own experience in parenting, as it is my four children's turn to be young adults, but I must say that I find it fascinating. Whenever I can, I try to attend meetings within my children's environment. Last year, for example, I took part in a series of meetings led by two people with great pedagogical experience: Andrzej Gorzkiewicz and Hanna Grzeskiewicz. They have created quite a lot of interesting and inquisitive workshops for parents. We were experiencing all kinds of problems, interesting opinions, and real emotions together. Why do adults not listen to children? Or why, on the other hand, do children not mind adults?

I find all of this fascinating, as I now seem to visit a completely different species. Those of us who are not grandparents yet perceive our children as extensions of us. In today's households, fathers are not as main figures as they used to be 50 or 60 years ago, but in many cases, they are still kind of the heavyweight; the source of the law, responsible for discipline – and what seems quite surprising – given that fatherly carefree, comfortable approach towards the children.

Mothers, on the other hand (although often portrayed as less neutral and worse guardians of peace within the home) seem to be the other way around – ready to participate in playing with children, undisturbed in the way we perceive Freud's Death Drive.

It could be said that the definition of what it means to be an adult differs from generation to generation as much as it differs from culture to culture. As an adolescent and young adult myself, I realize that my perception of adulthood might be quite different from that of my grandfather's. In this day and age, we are balancing between my generation that worries about becoming adults at the age of 26, and my father's generation, when it was abnormal for a 25-year-old to still be living in their parents' house. What is more, the structure of families has changed. We no longer live in houses where three or four generations of one family are under the same roof. Grandmothers and grandfathers, as they go sixty and older, do not expect their children to "start acting like adults" at the age of 25.

CHAPTER 7

Section 6: Balancing Work and Family Life

Lastly, we encourage employees to engage in sports and recreational activities as part of their personal and family lives outside of working hours. We have set up a leisure and games area within the premises. Employees can participate in and bond during various team-building and promotional activities. This includes Foosball, carom, chess, and various board games. To cater to employees' active natures, we also have a basketball hoop and a mini-golf area, for times when they need to take a short break to refresh. We give our employees the opportunity to live by the company's values when it comes to their personal and family lives, which are crucial in achieving an utmost work-life balance. We believe passionately that families are the bedrock of society and are the people whom we trust to inspire values, ethics, and characteristics of future generations. Therefore, we take steps to support our employees and their families who work together as one large family, collectively building a society that is enabled through this one family.

Most families these days are facing the dilemma of trying to balance work and family life. There's much to do in a limited amount of time. To help achieve this balance, Springboard provides its employees with flexible working hours to ensure flexibility in their work-life balance and optimization in family life as a priority. The employees will be able to stagger their working hours in accordance with their personal needs, with the option to come in an hour or two later or leave an hour or two earlier. This is particularly useful for employees with young children, who can stagger their working hours to match the pick-up and drop-off times for their children. It also enables staff to come to work relaxed and on time, with minimal stress from getting stuck in a traffic jam, and conclude work earlier and on time without feeling rushed. This flexibility also increases staff engagement and loyalty towards the company.

7.1. Prioritizing Family Time

Experienced parents will agree that there are few things greater than watching your child grow up into a good and decent person. It's no secret that children flourish when they have strong family relationships, but today's families are time-squeezed. To ensure some one-on-one family time, each month the Walters family holds "dates" with each parent-child combination. Prior to these special outings—whether it's biking at a park with a son or shopping and lunch with a daughter, whichever expression of love is appropriate—each child is given the opportunity to ask a parent, "When can I take you out on a date?" Not only is this scheduled event a cherished one-on-one time, but it also teaches the child how to take the initiative to plan and execute the "date"—providing lessons in respect, responsibility, and relationship development.

One of the most effective ways to share your family's values is through spending time together. In today's fast-paced society, it's common for family members to find themselves rushing from one activity to the next without taking the time to simply be together. It's important to be aware of how time is spent and to sit down and plan daily activities as a family. Use this guide to help prioritize family time, take the values quiz with your family, and practice activities that help you share your values with the family members you care about most.

7.2. Creating Work-Life Balance Strategies

Slowing down and finding time for the little things puts you on the path to work-life balance. Your calendar should be a "together" calendar, not an "individual" one. Make sure one-on-ones become family twos and family dinners become family four- or six-plusses. You want to spend time as a family, including extended family or friends, as much as possible. There are some cases where working parents celebrate weekends and sunsets, and children celebrate school breaks, meaning the importance of taking time to bond on these breaks is crucial. Creating more shared family moments during these breaks will increase personal happiness, and a happy life with others will lead to individual joy, as well. Work-life balance is about spending time together and enhancing quality time; the goal is to increase harmonious, shared experiences.

So, what are some things you can do to create work-life balance strategies for your household? Most importantly, celebrate being ordinary. Life is made up of small, mostly uncelebrated events, and being ordinary isn't boring, it's what holds us together. Take time to celebrate small accomplishments and each other. Regular celebrations increase human flourishing, which increases physical, emotional, and even financial health. In fact, celebrating ordinary events—like bedtime, wake-up time, and coming home—create a greater attachment with others and increased life satisfaction.

CHAPTER 8

Section 7: Overcoming Challenges and Adversities

When financial advisors are capable of providing sufficient reassurance, those who are anxiety-ridden and hopeless, resistant to help during times of duress, come forward and seek help. Speech within close-knit neighbor or friend circles ignites after many have sought help and were treated sensitively and successfully. Many people display resistance and hardly anyone cries voluntarily for help during times of adversity. For those who suffer apparent inadequacies when tested – while others appear entirely capable, their deficiencies are difficult to reveal. Perhaps pride plays a role in keeping us quiet during challenging times. Societal norms dictate what one should disclose to others. Sorting through emotional systems to find the root cause is a daunting challenge, and then to admit the root causes because they may appear irrational. It is virtually impossible to imagine being candid with others who would see you as inconsistently reasonable while you remain, ideally on the surface.

A significant part of financial planning is preparing for the unexpected. Many individuals have experienced hardships in life, some much more than others; however, all can share in similar situations, however different. As human beings, we all experience the same emotions related to circumstances beyond our control – overcoming challenges and adversities. Making life-altering financial decisions, often perceived as urgent, under such circumstances, can place an enormous additional burden on an individual or couple. Families may feel helpless and isolated. At some point, everyone will face a major challenge in their life. People cannot and should not go through it alone, especially when the concerns encompass financial decisions. Why then are so many people silent about these issues, accepting or perceiving that they are the only ones with a dilemma? Difficult times and the decisions that accompany the challenges are all part of the human experience.

8.1. Building Resilience and Perseverance

American Indians place great emphasis on the power of the family. Token gestures can never replace the reassurance of a parent, the wisdom of a grandparent, or the guidance of a child's extended family. Encouraging these connections and fostering our children's relationships with their family will transform one irreplaceable resource into several. By educating our children to appreciate a larger context for failure and success, parents can teach their children to thrive in an environment that is all too often volatile and cruel. When children fully expect to have the support of loving family members, they will grow in internal strength, and they will prosper beyond limits society would have otherwise set on them. With the investment of a supportive family, the fit will always be comfortable. With it, children will not fear the display of hard work and resilience.

The challenges young adults face today to become successful adults can seem overwhelming. Our culture is obsessed with finding the newest scientific method for raising our children. Many of us are looking for a magical tool to ensure our children will become adults who are resilient, confident, and successful. What resources do we already have to help our children along the way? A wealth of knowledge and wisdom can be found in American Indian proverbs. As you search for techniques and methods to make the impossible task of raising children a little easier, the foundation of American Indian philosophy can instead be used as a point of reference.

8.2. Supporting Each Other in Difficult Times

In addition to physical or practical support, families often need to spend time being supportive in helping each other cope with their feelings. We have explored the value of emotionally safe environments. In difficult times, families need to come together and help each member deal effectively with the sadness, fear, anger, or other negative emotions they are experiencing. They do this by listening, showing empathy, reassuring each other, offering emotional support, working through the concern together, and celebrating when the difficult time comes to an end. Part of providing valuable emotional support is helping family members grow their support network so that they will have more resources in future times of need.

There are few things as discouraging and as destructive as feeling you have no one to turn to in your dark times. Families need to support family members when they are facing difficulties. Children need to know that their families will be there to help when times get tough. This support is not simply moral support or kind words; it involves all family members working together to help solve problems. Hopefully, when the time comes, the family might also reach out to the larger community. While sharing their resources with those in need is a demonstration of a core family value, families also need to be willing to accept assistance when they need it. Accepting help from others can be difficult; often there are strings attached to the offer. However, friends and community members will also appreciate being asked to help and often rise to the occasion.

CHAPTER 9

Section 8: Sustaining the Legacy

The wealth of the family is not just financial, but includes the collective traits and interests the family holds dear. Family founders demonstrate moral legacies through their treatment of others and should be exemplars of integrity. Parents and grandparents must nurture the moral growth of their children and influence positive character traits to pass desirable values forward. Ultimately, the goal will be to have multiple generations internalize the original values initial generations hold as defining to the family's identity. It becomes vital to understand the moral power a family possesses in preserving and perpetuating its foundation of common values. Following generations should be educated about founding principles and about their responsibilities in preserving their family's heritage. Such understanding doesn't come naturally, and to ensure that the fabric of the family is strong enough to withstand turbulence, we recommend that families engage in coaching that enhances family leadership and ensures the successful development of future generations.

Sustaining a family legacy requires a never-ending commitment to maintaining a heritage and ensuring that values and traditions remain significant and relevant to future generations. While establishing a family structure and governing documents assists in the preservation of a legacy, maintenance is less about protecting the structure and more about preparing heirs to shoulder the responsibilities of keeping the legacy vibrant. Ongoing family leadership, commitment to learning, and open communication build a foundation for effective change and allow for freedom for individual aspirations.

9.1. Passing on Family Values to Future Generations

There are many times that the successful transfer of family values takes on forms more readily seen than those family portraits, tape recordings, or heirlooms. But the lasting memories and relationships with the characters in the stories read together, the words of the songs sung, and the life experiences lived will serve as a testament to these values. The values may even lie in cherished recipes, quilts, and crafts, the sense of humor, and the wisdom your family has preserved. These things may not guarantee success, respect, or good character easily. They can make these treasures real and enduring!

Another key point is to make sure that discussions are open and not judgmental. Rules for discussions are important, but it is also important to make sure that family members see and understand the distinction between right and wrong. Children should be encouraged to hold strong beliefs of love, respect, and compassion for others, fairness, respect for others' property, and the common good. Family traditions, customs, and histories are evidence of these values and beliefs.

It all starts with making a conscious effort to pass on family values to the younger individuals in the family. It is important to note that opportunities do not formally present themselves to have a formal classroom lesson. Many times, it is those spontaneous, impromptu gatherings that become the melting pot of ideas and thoughts. It is important for you to make sure that you at least openly express your ideas and beliefs so that they are known. With this in mind, it is important to make sure that you are always on guard to ensure that what you see and do does not send a different message than what you are trying to get across. Children may not do what they are told, but more often than not, they will do what they see.

9.2. Continuously Strengthening Family Bonds

As these children grow, they too would continue the legacy of fostering a strong family unit with strong values and moral ethics. With the positive upbringing from the family, these children would also seek life partners with similar aspirations, ensuring that the ever-growing family remains committed to uphold the family values for generations to come. As the family continues to grow through marriage, it is critical for parents to continuously encourage family awareness by fostering friendships among members of the entire extended family to establish rapport as we increase in both size and responsibilities to finally embrace the entire web of relationships within the family. This could come in the form of weddings, family-oriented gatherings, reunions, and honoring annual family traditions.

One of the identified critical success factors in nurturing family unity is the ongoing commitment to family time through bonding experiences to strengthen family relationships. As family-centric parents, these bonding sessions foster trust between family members and create a committed family unit to build a family consensus to adopt values and goals that are in the best interest of the family. There is a need to gradually encourage children to participate in these bonding sessions which also help children gather different perspectives of opinion that are contributing factors to their overall development. As the family grows in strength and wisdom, it is only competent that they initiate community projects that can leverage the strengths of its members to better the community. Here we can see the family stepping into the role of a true leader, walking the talk by shouldering responsibility of their community where they are just one of the many families and are contributing to a greater cause.

CHAPTER 10

Conclusion

One of the best examples of the importance of family business contribution to the wealth and social welfare for the good citizenship we have today around the world began with the Dutch East India Company (1602-1799), aligned to the collective interests of the administrators, the investors, and the monarchy. Over time, after the 2000s, at a time of global financial crisis and the rise of emerging countries, the capitalist system turned to the economic role of national and transnational family companies. Once this doctrine of economic and financial markets, everyday activities, and families, their traditions, objectives, spirit, and values, which compromise future generations and the global social welfare, influenced by legislative rules and "good practices" guides.

This article was written based on the results of a qualitative research analyzing the characteristics of Brazilian, Colombian, Italian, Mexican, and Spanish family companies and entrepreneurs. It revealed details on the family values and human relations practices according to the perceptions of the family and non-family members of the council. The conclusions come from these results, as well as from the authors' understanding about entrepreneurship and family business management resulting from previous research, PhD in this theme, and publications in this field. Therefore, the authors register that there are more questions than great answers, given research limitations that do not intend to subordinate the conducted research. Nevertheless, because of this approach, whether in family business or in whatever area or field, the research process is found here as an answer full of significance about life and human values around family relations for business management.